# Sex: The Sex Guide for Couples

## Have More Intimacy, More Passion and an Amazing Sex Life

# Table of Contents

# Introduction

I want to thank you and congratulate you for downloading the book, *"Sex: The Ultimate Sex Guide for Couples - Have More Intimacy, More Passion and an Amazing Sex Life"*.

This book will teach you how to supercharge your intimacy, rekindle the passion, and enhance your sex life.

Sex is the grease that keeps the wheels of romantic relationships turning smoothly. Without it, you will undoubtedly have a hard time having the happiness that you've always wanted in your romantic relationship. When you start going out, you probably find it impossible to resist each other. In fact, you are likely to do crazy sexual things in the park or on your evening commute. When you think about him or her, your heart races and you cannot just wait for the next moment you see him or her.

Well, if only this fire could keep burning for the rest of your life, sexless relationships wouldn't exist and cases of having to seek sexual release outside your relationship won't even exist. Unfortunately, there seems to be a bug that catches many couples in long-term relationships. Sex starts diminishing and it isn't uncommon to hear couples confess that they have sex once a month or just a couple of times a year.

Then you might wonder; what really happened that makes him or her less attracted to you sexually? And what can you do to change the situation? Well, this book will help you to understand all that and help you skyrocket your sex life.

Even if the passion is there, but you just want to take your relationship to a higher level, this book is for you. I share with you some fun and exciting ways to help you discover how to have more intimacy and passion in your relationship for an amazing sex life. Read on and enjoy sprucing up your relationship.

Thanks again for downloading this book, I hope you enjoy it!

information is without contract or any type of guarantee assurance.

The trademarks that are used are without any consent, and the publication of the trademark is without permission or backing by the trademark owner. All trademarks and brands within this book are for clarifying purposes only and are the owned by the owners themselves, not affiliated with this document.

# Sex: What Makes Your Spouse Not Want You in Bed Like Before?

There's a good and bad side to everything. Even long-term relationships have their downsides and perks. Being in an intimate relationship can be the best thing that ever happened to you. However, when things get comfortable, you might be headed for the drains.

Intimacy and sex becomes very rare when a relationship gets too comfortable. In fact, you might find yourselves having only obligatory sex once in awhile, in the missionary position only, where the man is always on top. Afterwards, you both toss over and fall asleep.

Undoubtedly, it is not easy to keep things heated in the bedroom; it takes some little effort that very few are willing to take. Although it is okay for you to be comfortable, sex plays an essential role in building relationships and strengthening them.

With regular sex and intimacy, you do not just get mental and physical health benefits, but also strengthen the bond between you and your spouse. If your relationship feels a bit boring, stagnant and lacking the passion, it needs to drive it, you need to do a few things to reignite the love.

Well, before you can reignite that fire, the first thing you need to do is to understand why your sex life seems to have taken a nosedive. Since men and women are quite different, perhaps understanding what has made him or her lose interest in sex can help you to come up with a workable solution. Let's start with him then move on to her. What makes your man not have as much sex as you did when you first started? If your spouse does not want you in bed like before, here are some reasons why:

# Him

## Andropause

Just as women go through menopause, men also undergo andropause. However, male 'menopause' is less intense and not as sudden as the hormonal changes in women. Your man can experience a decreased sex drive if he is going through this phase of his life. You can discuss your sexual feelings to find a way out.

## Pornography

Although watching a little pornography can help spice your sex lives, too much of it can tear your relationship apart. Addiction to pornography can cause your husband to resort to porn for stimulation and satisfaction instead of relying on you. He develops unrealistic expectations of you that when you fail to meet, leads to his lack of satisfaction.

If he spends too much time alone on the computer or has become less interested in being physical with you, it could be that he is into porn. You can talk to him about it or seek professional help.

## Low Levels of Testosterone

Hypogonadism, a condition brought about by low testosterone levels in your man's body could be the reason he does not want as much sex as before. Some signs to look out for are low libido, low mood, decreased energy, muscle mass loss, fatigue, and erectile dysfunction. Do not worry because more than 13 million men in America suffer from this condition and it can be treated.

## Insufficient Kisses and Hugs

Your relationship needs a lot of physical contact to sustain your libido and keep the sex alive. If you do not make your man feel wanted, and fail to shower him with lots of kisses and hugs, he is likely to lose his libido. You can try to surprise him with kisses and hugs, when he less expects it; it can make a difference in your sex lives, let alone his happiness.

## An Underlying Medical Condition

You man's low libido could be a sign of an underlying medical problem, such as prostate cancer, diabetes, or even heart disease. You can talk to him about it, and maybe get him to see a doctor.

## Allergies

Various studies link allergies to decrease in sexual satisfaction and drive. If your man sneezes, sniffles, or even coughs, his libido and mood for sex can be affected. Help him see a doctor to prescribe drugs to help cure his allergies.

## A Bad Economy

A bad economy can subject your man to stress, which can temporarily lower his sex drive. You might not stop the financial problems your relationship is facing, but you can prepare him a nice lean dinner or exercise with him to help lower his stress levels. When he starts feeling better, his sex drive might also increase, especially once endorphins are released into his blood stream during the exercises.

## Masturbation

Masturbation subjects men to a higher level of sexual stimulation of more intensity than what a vagina can offer. If your man gets used to this level of sexual satisfaction, he might not get satisfied with what you can give him. You can make it a policy that whenever he is in the mood, you should be his only way to orgasm.

## Medications

Certain medications are known to lower sexual libido. If your man is under any kind of medication, it could be the reason he has a low sex drive.

# Her

## Medication

Just like in the case of men, medication can lower your woman's sex drive. Hormonal contraceptives can also lower her libido. You can opt for condoms, IUDs or diaphragms, as they do not use hormones.

## Bed Not Sexy

Bringing technology into the bedroom is a major cause of low libido in the modern world as it causes distraction, hence making sex initiation very difficult. TVs, newspapers, phones, laptops, etc, should not find their way into your bedroom or bed. You can also give sex a priority in your lives.

## Busy Life

Just like men, having a busy life can subject women to stress, which in turn can cause hormonal changes in their bodies. This can explain why she is no longer interested in making love to you. You need to make sex a priority in your lives, and go for spontaneous sex surprises. Helping her relax her mind and body through exercise can also help kickoff her libido.

## She Does Not Like Her Body

If she doesn't like her body for whatever reason, her drive for sex will definitely be low. You need to make her feel good about herself by complimenting her. You can be sure to get her in the mood if you compliment her often.

## Menopause

The hormonal changes that occur in a woman's body can lower her libido. If your woman is going through this phase of her life, expect her sex drive to decrease.

## You are Not Interested

If you show disinterest in your woman, her sex drive will go down. You need to show interest in her always.

## Stress or Depression

Just like men, women experience low libido when stressed or depressed. If your wife is undergoing any form of stress or depression, her sex drive will go down. You need to help her manage the stress. Engaging her in daily exercises would be a perfect way to start getting her in the mood.

## She's into Toys

If your woman is addicted to masturbation using toys, such as the vibrator, she might not find you good enough. Although using a vibrator once in awhile can supercharge your sex life, she should not be addicted to using it.

So, now that you know what has been bothering him or her, what can you do to get them to become the horny self they used to be when they are around you? Given that men are different from women, what turns on women is very different from what turns on men. In the next chapter, we will discuss just how to get him in the mood then move on to discuss how to get her in the mood.

# How to Get Him in the Mood

Although your man could not take his hands off you when you first met, he might seem not in the mood after awhile. He might get distracted once in awhile and look somehow off, hence the need for you to get him in the mood. Despite the fact that most men easily get in the mood for sex, yours might seem a bit off on some days.

These tips should help you get him back in the mood for hot sexual sessions:

### Prepare Him Bubble Bath

When your man comes back home from work after a long day's work, you can welcome him with a candle-lit bubble bath scented with vanilla. Various studies indicate that men get aroused the most by the smell of vanilla. You can take it a notch higher by waiting for him naked in the tab with two glasses of wine.

### Give Him a Sensual Massage

You can give him a sensual massage to arouse his feelings and get him in the mood. Use things like fluffy wool or feathers or silky scarves to gently flip all over his body. Cinnamon scented candle and massage oils like frankincense and lavender are perfect for the sensual massage session. You can add more vigor to the massage by blindfolding your man.

### Whisper Sexy Words in His Ears

When around him, whisper sexy words in his ears while letting him feel your deep breaths. You can also leave him a sexy voice message in your sexiest voice.

## Look Him Directly in the Eyes

Enhance intimacy and arouse your man by staring directly into his eyes; do not blink or break your gaze. Well, don't just stare at him; use lustful eyes to lock your eyes with his and you will see how turned on he is. Men go crazy at the thought of a horny woman. If you could tell him that you are not wearing anything down there, his lust for you will go on overdrive.

## Sing Him a Love Song

Choose one of your man's favorite love songs that you also like. Record yourself singing it and save it on a CD. Leave it on his car seat so he can find it in the morning as he leaves for work. When he gets to listen to it, he won't stop thinking about you throughout the day. He will be eager to come back home and share good intimate moments with you.

## Express Your Feelings through Poetry

Write either a traditional or naughty poem about what you love about your man, your love life or even the first time you met. Leave it somewhere open where he will find it, or just read it to him. You can do the reading in bed.

## Find the Way to His Heart

They say one of the ways to a man's heart is through good food. Prepare his favorite dish and place a sexy note next to the serving, letting him know your expectations of him later in the evening or night.

## Give Him Flowers

According to a certain study conducted by the University of Rutgers, most men love receiving flowers, it increases their happiness and interactions socially. Choose his favorite colors or send him a bouquet of blue, red and purple flowers with the scents he loves most. Deliver the flowers with a sexy note.

## Buy Him a Gift

Surprise your man with a gift you are sure he will love. You can also ask him to accompany you to a lingerie store and help you select something that he would love to see you wear.

## Share a Bar of Chocolate

Studies associate chocolate with less depression and loneliness in men. You can also choose a menu that features chocolates to share with your man. There are several online that you can try.

## Deep-throat Him

Your man will definitely love the feeling of his penis deep in your throat. You can start by sucking his not erect penis until it is hard before you can deep-throat him. If this is something you cannot do, you can give him a visual effect by deep throating a toy penis.

## Shave or Wax for Him

Men love the soft feel of smooth skin. Rub his penis gently against rough areas of your skin and slowly move to the smooth shaven or waxed areas so he can feel the difference in touch. You should do this firmly and lightly until he is so hard that he begs to feel the warmth of your vagina.

## Nibble the Back of His Neck

Arouse the sexual desire in your man by nibbling the back of his neck using your tongue. Letting him feel your deep breaths is a plus.

## Give Him a Spicy Kiss

Apply a spicy lipstick on your lips before kissing your man. It will spice up your oral sex sessions. He will get stimulated while you enjoy using your hot lips on him.

## Rub His Penis

Gently hold your man's penis with your fingers and gently rub him. You can apply some lotion or gel to reduce friction and facilitate the arousal.

## Get him to dress you

A horny man is a very creative one and will spend any amount of money to get his sexual fantasies met. Give your man a chance to dress you from head to toe for an entire week and see what happens. Let him do the shopping for the stuff that he wants you to wear. He will love it when you follow what he says. And the thought that you are wearing the clothes that he bought you will make him want you even the more. He will be looking forward for a wonderful session when he sees you.

## Make the First Move

When you know he is about to get home, get naked and spread yourself on the bed waiting for him. His first sight of you will definitely arouse him and get him in the mood. You can also take the first step during other times, for instance, when you relaxing in the living room over the weekend. You can move closer to him and start kissing him; he will definitely respond. Just ensure that he is in a good mood before making the move.

You can also undress him and push him onto the bed before you take charge and do the riding. You can also give him a quickie, look good for him, give him blowjobs, spank his butt, get him ready from the moment he wakes up, and stimulate his senses to get him in the mood.

# How To Get Her In The Mood

According to two psychology professors at the Texas University and co-authors of the book 'Why Women Have Sex: Understanding Sexual Motivations from Adventure to Revenge', women need to be inspired in order to get in the mood for sex, whereas men are up for it anywhere and anytime, irrespective of the prevailing situation.

Men often wish that their women would respond more to their sexual gestures, or even initiate sex more. This difference is attributed to the fact that women's desire for sex depends on their immediate environment in terms of response and variance. Women experience sex in both their bodies and minds; men, on the other hand, focus more on their genitals.

Men are compared to firemen, who are ready to have sex anytime because to them, it is an emergency. Women, however, are exciting just like fire; the surrounding conditions must be right for them to fire up, let alone keep burning.

Your woman wants to have sex only when she thinks it is worth it. Therefore, you need to motivate your wife or girlfriend, for them to see sex as an exciting priority. Here are some ways to help you get her in the mood:

## Give Her Mild Bondage

Your woman can be turned on by the mere thought that you are entirely responsible for her satisfaction sexually. You can get her ready by sending her an email, or leaving a voice message or note earlier in the day. Tell her to put on some make up and wear your favorite outfit.

If you love a submissive woman, you can order her to submit to you by getting her on her knees and being your 'slave' just for the moment. Be her master and order her to do what you want. You can also use a gentle item to tie her as bondage and use a tickler or feather to arouse her.

You can also opt for gentle bondage sex toys or just spank her lightly using your hand. Note that the aim of the bondage is to bring your woman pleasure so that she can climax; no kind of pain or humiliation should be involved.

## Role Play

You can ask her to role play her fantasy or be the slut you always yearn for. You can ask her to play the role of a stripper and give you one of a kind show. If she is okay with having a camera around, you can decide to record the show for future use and reference.

## Make Her Mind Sex

For women, sex starts in the mind. Your woman cannot think of having sex with you if she has other things occupying her mind. Tell her what you want to do to her in advance in detail. When together, rub your hands against her body and kiss her shoulders up her neck.

Remove her panties with her clothes on and slip your hand beneath her dress or top to tease her nipples. You can use the other hand to gently touch and rub her butt. You can let her arouse herself as you watch by rubbing her clit; let her sit on a chair with legs apart.

You can ask her to describe how she feels and before you know it, she will be begging you to do that to her, but with your hard penis deep inside her vagina.

## Explore Her Fantasies

You can ask your woman to give you details of her sexual fantasies. By just sharing that kind of information with you, she will automatically get aroused. However, you need to prepare for the unexpected as her fantasy or what turns her on might make you insecure; there is no need for that.

Take advantage of that opportunity for your own gain. You can tell her story that matches her fantasy as you caress and kiss her gently. Whisper softly in her ears and let her imagination be her only limitation. If she responds to it, you can be sure that she is getting wet as well.

## Watch Passionate Porn Together

Unlike men, women prefer aural porn. Find a suitable one with a sexy storyline and enjoy listening together. A passionate visual erotica would do though if you can find one. As you get aroused watching or listening to your favorite erotica, you can run your hands inside her clothes for greater arousal and pleasure.

## Make Compliments

Women love compliments mainly because they are more self-conscious regarding their nude bodies and easily get insecure than their male counterparts. You need to make your woman feel secure in order to get her in the mood.

As you caress her body and give her hot kisses, tell her that you find her attractive, what you like most about her body, and how much she turns you on; and, you just can't keep your hands and tongue off her body. The more specific your compliments about her are the better.

You can tell her you love her soft skin, warm smile, beautiful shape or even size, and the soft feel of her firm breasts. Actually, the more you compliment her daily, the more she will always be in the mood.

## Kiss Her Passionately

It takes experience to be a great kisser. You can begin by just licking her gently and just letting her enjoy the feel of your tongue against her body. Lick her lips with your tongue's tip as you gently open your mouth for deeper kissing. Always remember to be gentle and avoid biting her, even by mistake.

Remember to keep your breath fresh before kissing; brush your teeth or chew fresh mint gum beforehand. Supercharge her sex drive and strengthen the bond between you and her by maintaining eye contact whilst kissing her; you must not close your eyes.

## Caress Her Sensually

You can easily get your woman in the mood by simply giving her tender strokes of your touches all over her body. As you touch her, your aim is to get her aroused for intercourse. Use long gentle caresses to massage her breasts and touch her all over. You can also move your hands down her body and put your hand in her panties to gently rub her clit.

Maintain the slow tempo throughout until she is totally aroused. Only then can you play rough, as she would be asking for.

## Prolong the Foreplay

Foreplay means the world to women. Do not just rip off her panties and expect her to let you penetrate. You need to engage her in prolonged foreplay before you can make love to her. Hold her close, stroke her hair, touch her face, look directly into her eyes, kiss her soft spots, caress her body, and even kiss her neck.

You can also give her a sensual massage as part of foreplay to arouse her properly. The gentle touch of your fingertips all over her body, commonly known as 'spider legs' can get your woman really wet, ready for intercourse.

## Create a Good Ambience

The right ambience to a woman is as good as being in the mood. You need to ensure that the ambience is stress-free, has proper lighting, is quiet, and if possible, smells great. The environment should also be clean because your woman will definitely love that.

It is easier for you to get her in the mood if the ambience is good because it relaxes and calms her mind to focus only on the feelings you are trying to arouse in her.


Now that you understand your man or woman and probably have a good idea what is likely to turn them on, the next step is ensuring that you don't ruin the session when you get to have one. And in so doing, you can be sure that there will be a next one.

# Crazy Ways to Supercharge Every Session

The fact that you do not have sex with your spouse is reason enough to kill the passion despite the underlying causes. However, these great yet crazy ways will help supercharge every session.

Here are a few tips to get you going:

## Engage in Cyber-sex and Watch Porn Together

If your spouse lives away, long distance can make it hard to keep the bond intact, as you cannot get to have sex as much as you would want. You can agree to engage in cyber sex as often as you can. However, even if you live under the same roof, you can take advantage of online porn to improve your intimacy and how often you have sex.

There are several female-friendly porn videos online designed specifically for couples like you dealing with a sexless relationship. It does not have to be anything crude, which can be a turn-off for most women. You can watch porn together before some sessions to prepare your bodies for the awaiting hot action.

## Explore Your Fantasies

Everyone has a sexual fantasy if not many. Sit with your spouse and discuss your sexual fantasies. If possible, write them on separate pieces of paper or notebook pages. You can set a day for exploring the fantasies, or just make it spontaneous.

On that day, you pick a paper containing a fantasy randomly from the jar where you keep them and explore it together with your spouse. You can make it a habit to explore a single fantasy during every session.

## Don't Forget to Touch/Foreplay

There is power in touching your spouse gently and lovingly. A hug, massage, caresses, or even slipping your arm around your spouse might be all you need to arouse them. These small gestures can help strengthen the bond between the two of you, in addition to boosting your affectionate feelings.

Before engaging in penetrative sex during any session, ensure that you foreplay for long, kiss, caress and cuddle each other to arouse yourselves.

## Multiple Orgasms

Although spontaneous sex is exciting, can help kill boredom and arouse feelings of passion, multiple orgasms are just as important. No matter how busy you might be, you need to schedule enough time for you and your spouse to orgasm simultaneously. If possible, you can place this at the top of your busy schedule.

However, be sure to make this a habit if you want to maintain the right intimacy level and satisfaction in your relationship. Every session should feature multiple organisms for both you and your spouse.

## Build Anticipation when Apart

Do not let the sex stop the moment you part ways. You can keep it alive by using technology. You can communicate throughout the day even when apart through text, email or even social media platforms like Facebook.

Send your spouse sexy messages to arouse their curiosity, hence the anticipation to get back home later for great fun times together.

Just a tip: you can tell your man how you forgot to wear panty so you can hit it right on later, when you get back home.

This can get your partner really aroused while still away, ushering the beginning of a hot session later. When they get home, they might want to start making love right from the moment they get through the door.

**Break up the Sex Routine**

You need to shake things up and break the routine you and your spouse have developed of just having sex in the bedroom, on your bed. Try a new place for every session. The bathroom showers, bath tabs, against walls, back seat of your car, kitchen counters, or even living room floors are perfect places for having a quickie.

If you are the couple that loves publicity or being outdoors, a private beach would be perfect for that steamy sex you haven't had in awhile. What about a quickie in a public washroom? Well, it is all about the amount of risk your adrenaline can handle; that's what makes the sex even more exciting. Just be creative.

When you get the time to connect with your spouse, you build up the passion needed for steamy lively sex.

**Different Sex Positions**

Have you tried out all the different sex positions out there? Well, they are so many that you cannot exhaust them all. You need to make trying out different sex positions a policy in your relationship. I wrote a book with 25 sex positions that will supercharge your sex life; you can search it on Kindle Store.

You might be surprised how much excitement a new sex position can bring into your sexless relationship, arousing so much passion to keep it alive. Check out the last chapter for some of the sex positions you can try out to help reignite the passion in your love life.

Try a new position during every session to supercharge it.

**Embrace Sex Toys**

Using sex toys during a sex session with your spouse can supercharge each session that you have. There are toys for men and those for women, such as vibrators and artificial vaginas.

There are several online stores selling various toys you can consider. Visit some of them with your spouse and make orders for local delivery. You will be surprised how toys can supercharge and change your sex lives for the better.

**Oral Sex**

Oral sex is just as good as penetrative sex, or even better. You can consider giving each other some good oral sex. Men love their penis being sucked and teased. You can suck your man until he cums in your mouth; the decision to swallow the sperms or not is entirely yours.

Women also love having their clits sucked and licked. Place a pillow below your waist and another beneath your man's chest so he can have good access of your clit for some good sucking.

When sucking your man, you can consider applying your favorite ice cream flavor and licking it all off after taking a sip of hot coffee. Get down on your knees and give him the blowjob of his life for that crazy session. Sounds crazy, but your man will love it.

## Talk Dirty

Tell your man how you love feeling his size and hardness deep inside you. Men love to hear how good they are at giving you pleasure. Moan (but don't fake it) when he is making love to you. Call out his name and tell him to give it to you harder, deeper, and faster.

## Top-up Massage with Heated Sex

Give your man a good massage. Start with his back and let him turn over. Massage his whole body except his penis, giving him the urge for more and more of your touch. Gently massage the areas around his penis before giving his penis a soft yet arousing massage.

Rub him gently until he ejaculates, or tosses you over for one good love making session.

## Drink Wine

Various studies have linked sexual satisfaction in both men and women to wine. You can consider starting each session with a glass of wine for ultimate fulfillment of your sexual needs and desires.

**Incorporate Purple into Your Décor**

According to a study recently carried out in Britain, you can make your sex lives more active by incorporating purple into your interior décor. You could spread your bed with purple beddings or have purple fabric on your living room furniture.

Wearing purple or red lingerie earlier before your session can only excite your partner, preparing them for the great times ahead.

**Stop taking statins medications**

Some of these include fluvastatin, pitavastatin, atorvastatin, simvastatin, rosuvastatin, pravastatin etc and are marketed under such brand names like Crestor, Lipitor, Lipostat and Lescol. These could lower your sex drive. They are usually designed to lower cholesterol levels in your bloodstream but they have many side effects.

# Eat For Sex

What you eat has a profound effect on how you act or perform in different facets of your life. Just as there are foods meant to boost your immunity, fight inflammation, lose weight, enhance your mental functioning etc, some foods have been proven to help you get into the right mood for sex with greater ease. We will learn about some of these:

## Pesto

This has been known to enhance sex drive in women thanks to the effects of pine nuts, which are high in zinc. Women who have high zinc levels are often likely to have a high sex drive. Zinc is actually the ingredient responsible for aphrodisiac effects that are in oysters but spaghetti even do better.

## Grilled cheese

A study conducted by Skout showed that 32% of those who take grilled cheese regularly (at least 6 times a month) have greater sex drive.

## Banana

Banana has high levels of tyrosine, which helps in the production of dopamine and norepinephrine.

## Cheese and other dairy products

These are high in proteins, which contain amino acids, which in turn help in the production of dopamine.

## Watermelon

This one has been proven to increase male libido. But if you can find the tiger penis (Chinese), you will even be in greater luck. The fruit has high lycopene levels. Lycopene rivals Viagra in its ability to enhance relaxation of blood vessels and enhance circulation in the right places.

## Chocolate

This does wonders for everyone; men and women, given that it increases the production of dopamine and serotonin.

## Pomegranate Spritzer

This one has been proven to enhance arousal in men.

## Coffee and decaf

Coffee will help your woman get in the mood while decaf will help you (the man) get into the mood.

## Eat herbs that increase your sex drive

Some of the well known herbs for this include:

Kava: This one will give you a tingling, slightly numbing, and pleasant sensation upon touch making you yearn for sex. It works for both men and women.

Kratom

Ginseng

Wild dagga: This one enhances blood flow all over your body and increases sensitivity.

Kanna

Damiana

# Top 5 Sex Positions to Try Out

These 5 sex positions can help enhance your sex life, supercharging every session for climax and multiple orgasms.

## Bootyful View

Let your man sit on the bed with his legs horizontally apart, each toward a different foot of your bed. With your back facing him, stretch your legs on either of his sides towards his back. Lower yourself and let his penis enter your vagina. Relax your body torso right between his legs. Using his feet as your support, ride him, sliding your body up and down.

This position is perfect if your man is an Aries; they are known for being aggressive and having an eye for rough, fast sex. You get to control the depth, speed, and intensity of penetration as he enjoys the view of your booty.

## The Missionary

Oh! He is a Taurus? Then he will love the missionary style because of his sensuality and love for slow sex. A poll reported that 21% of Americans preferred this position.

It does not have to be boring. Moreover, you can be sure that your woman will love having you on top. She gets maximum pleasure in addition to seeing your vigor and stamina. Having your weight all on her, she will enjoy the intimacy and closeness that comes with this position.

For optimal pleasure whilst stimulating her clitoris, go at it diagonally. All she has to do is lie back with legs apart. Gain penetration and start your diagonal ride towards pleasure.

Tip: You can try some variations of the missionary style for added pleasure.

## Girl-on-top/Cowgirl

This position gives your woman control over her orgasm. It is perfect if she is sensual yet loves rough sex. She also controls the speed and depth of penetration. Apart from your penis getting to hit her exposed clitoris for maximum pleasure, she works out her quads and calves for a fitter body.

This is the opposite of the bootyful view position. You sit with your legs apart and let her sit on your laps facing you. Let her legs stretch on each of your sides towards your back. She gently lets your penis penetrate into her vagina.

With her knees up and hands on the bed for support, she moves her butt up and down for maximum penetration. She is the boss, so let her take charge. Just sit back and enjoy the pleasure.

## Spooning

Spooning is intimate and romantic, let alone comfortable. It is the perfect position for that lazy Sunday afternoon. You both lie on bed facing each other. Get close and cross your legs.

Hold each other close as he reaches your vagina for penetration. You can enjoy the slow ride as you hold each other tight and exchange passionate kisses. This position is also perfect if you are pregnant.

As he rubs the front of your vagina (where most of nerves are found) using his hard penis, you can expect to get a lot of pleasure.

## Doggy Style

Which man would not like the doggy style? Your man will. Kneel on the edge of your bed with legs apart. Lower your torso and use your hands to support yourself on the bed. Let him penetrate your vagina and give you pleasure. Both your G-spot and clitoris are within reach for optimal stimulation.

You can take turns in taking control. You can also move your body back and forth for greater penetration. Your man can hold your hips to help maintain the stamina. Just relax your mind and enjoy.

# Conclusion

Thank you again for downloading this book!

I hope that this book has empowered you with the right skills and knowledge you need to bring back passion to fire up your relationship.

The next step is to try what you've just learnt.


Finally, if you enjoyed this book, would you be kind enough to leave a review for this book on Amazon?

Check out my other book on Amazon!

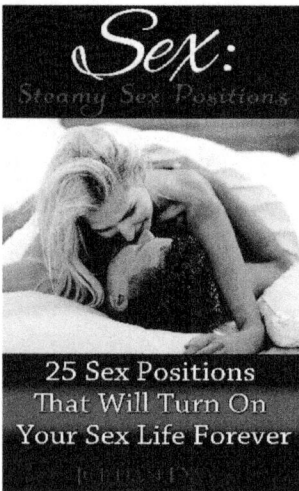

Thank you and good luck!

Printed in Great Britain
by Amazon